HOW I FOUND
PEACE, JOY, AND HAPPINESS
IN A WORLD OF INSANITY

An Artist Reflects on his Catholic Faith

ANTHONY QUARTUCCIO

Copyright © 1995 by Anthony Quartuccio

ALL RIGHTS RESERVED

Library of Congress Catalog Number 94-92017

ISBN 0-9606934-3-2

First Printing

Printed in the United States of America

Other books by the author:

Tony's Guide to Better Painting
Rambling Through Baja California With Pen & Brush
Santa Clara Valley — An Artist's View Today & Yesterday
Saints of the California Landscape — by Raymund Wood
    (Illustrated by Anthony Quartuccio)

All art work by author.
Photos by author except where credit is given.
Book production by Cypress House, Fort Bragg, CA 95437

Biblical quotations from the Bible
Excerpts are taken from the **New American Bible With Revised New Testament** Copyright © 1986 and the **New American Bible With Revised Psalms** Copyright © 1991 by the Confraternity of Christian Doctrine, 3211 Fourth Street, N.E., Washington D.C. 20017-1194 and are used with permission. All rights reserved.

Reference — Baltimore Catechism No. Two
Confraternity of Christian Doctrine
Washington D.C.

Anthony Quartuccio
24 Almond Crest Court
Paso Robles, CA 93446-5202

HOW I FOUND

PEACE, JOY, AND HAPPINESS

IN A WORLD OF INSANITY

DEDICATED TO THE HONOR AND GLORY OF GOD

and to

Our Lady of Guadalupe

ACKNOWLEDGMENTS

I wish to acknowledge my thankfulness to the many people who have helped me to put together this book. First, to Almighty God, the Father, the Son and the Holy Spirit, for without His grace, I could not even have begun; to my wife Maria, for her support in all that I do; and to my son Anthony, for his many suggestions. Most of all, I am grateful to Kim Blythe, who helped me with the computer typing.

The following people contributed with suggestions, corrections, and advice in the process of editing the manuscript: Maisie Egger, Father James Henry, Janet Victor, John Fremont, and Father George Twigg-Porter S.J., M.A. To the countless people who offered me encouragement, I give my sincere thanks.

I also wish to thank
The Most Reverend
SYLVESTER D. RYAN, D.D.
Bishop of Monterey

and, especially,

to my wife

MARIA BARO QUARTUCCIO

For her love that encouraged me to write this book.

TABLE OF CONTENTS

Preface	7
The Divine Artist	9
Nature — Awe of God's Creation	14
Seeking God	17
A Cry for God	20
Ways to God	22
Christ — My Model	25
The Sermon on the Mount	31
Faith — A gift from God	32
Christ's Church	35
The Church is Indestructible	43
A Summary of Faith	46
Means of Holiness — The Sacraments	53
In Touch With God — The Mass	60
Receiving Christ — Holy Communion	63
A Day of Happiness	65
Never Alone — The Blessed Sacrament	70
My Guardian Angel	74
The Saints	76
Prayer and Meditation	86
Guide to True Happiness	88
Attaining Happiness	90
A String of Beads	92
Death	94
Who Is My Neighbor?	100
The Mural — Holy Cross Church	103
My Goal — God in Heaven	114
Epilogue	118

"ALWAYS BE READY TO GIVE AN EXPLANATION TO ANYONE WHO ASKS YOU FOR A REASON FOR YOUR HOPE." (1 PETER 3:15)

PREFACE

There comes a time in life when one reflects on the innermost character of one's mind, actions, and feelings. My happiness can perhaps shed some sunshine upon others who are wandering aimlessly, seeking to grasp some way of life. I want to share the faith that lives in me; it is the sole source of my peace, joy, and happiness.

A society without God is a world of insanity. God leaves men and women to their own selfishness when they drift away from Him, resulting in the destruction of self and values.

I firmly believe that the Catholic faith is true. The modern world seems to look down on one who is committed to possession of the truth. In the midst of uncertainty about conflicting philosophies of life, I reaffirm the solemn words of Christ Himself: *"I am the way and the truth and the life."* (John 14:6)

In the following pages I want to publicly give thanks and gratitude to Almighty God for the faith I cherish. I want to give the reasons for my faith. God's grace has brought me a happy heart and deep appreciation of His love.

This book is not intended to be an artistic work. It is a sincere outpouring of my soul about the faith that guides me. It is about the light and foundation of my life. This is my road map on the journey to eternity.

Anthony Quartuccio

Painting the mural at Holy Cross Church.

Photo by Father Nalin

THE DIVINE ARTIST

Peace! Joy! Happiness! What beautiful words!

While painting in my studio in San Jose one dark and gloomy morning, I asked myself a serious question: What is the source of my peace, joy, and happiness; what is the power that moves me daily in a world of unhappiness?

I looked out the window of my small art gallery and watched a heavy rain storm drench East Santa Clara Street. A blustering wind swept newspapers through the air, creating a depressing scene. In spite of the dreary weather outside, my heart was light and cheerful. I lifted my mind upward and thanked God for giving me the wonderful gift of painting. I began to reflect on myself, the meaning of life, and the principles I believe in.

I reflected on many things while painting a mural for my parish church. In the process of painting it, I meditated deeply about God, Christ, His Church, and the world. In doing so, I found how tremendously important were the truths that I live by in my Catholic faith.

In the depths of my soul, I had a need to express my thoughts and feelings, to use paint and to create something of beauty on canvas. I wanted to set down some of my impressions of God's beautiful world and show the relationship between the physical and the spiritual that I see in the things around me.

The subjects an artist paints are a reflection of himself, his mind and his spirit. They are also reflections of his love and emotions. I see God's creative power manifested in nature. All I need to do is observe and try to translate what I see. I toy with an idea, then think, plan, and execute it on a blank canvas with a palette knife. It may be a mountain scene, a mood, a story or an experience that inspires a painting, but there is always something of myself in it.

In my painting, I am not perfect. I try to do better each time. How wonderful is the perfect artistry of God's creation, originating in His mind and simply willed into existence.

I began to reason. If I can make my images from concrete reality, imagine what God creates out of nothing! I sat and pondered this great truth.

I observed that there is order governing everything. When I am drawing or painting a subject, I find there are certain rules to follow if I want to be a successful artist. I study nature, physical laws, balance, and composition, and I learn from these. The laws that govern shadows, perspective, or folds in a dress do not limit freedom, but give credibility to the painting. Likewise, my life is governed by rules for human behavior: The TEN COMMANDMENTS. Rather than restricting my freedom, observing them leads to order, peace, and happiness. They are God's directions for my soul.

As color, harmony, balance, and composition are essential to a fine painting, so are the commandments absolutely necessary for human conduct. Disobeying the rules of painting results in a bad painting. So, too, my life will result in sin when I deliberately ignore and disobey even one of the commandments. This leads to unhappiness, despair and, ultimately, eternal damnation.

The artist at work.

Yes, God is the Divine Artist, and man is His marvelous creation. He created me — a being composed of matter and spirit. I am one of His paintings, as yet unfinished. I look at myself and I am astonished at the gifts He has given me: my eyes, my ears, my feet, my hands, my beating heart, this complex bundle of flesh and blood! Furthermore, He gave me a mind, body and soul. Most important, He gave me intellect and free will.

God loved me enough to will my existence into the vastness of all eternity. He thought of me, or He would not have created me through my father and mother. Out of millions of possible genetic combinations, only one became me, Anthony!

Here I am, myself, and no one else. There is no copy of me. I am an original among the billions and trillions of people He created and is still creating. So it is with each of us, no two are exactly alike. We are individuals, and He knows every detail that makes us what we are. God makes no mistakes.

In God's great painting of the universe, He has a special place for me. He has a personal interest in all that I do. Nothing escapes Him. There is a reason for my existence. It all fits into His eternal plan. I may not know the reason, but it is up to me to do His will to the best of my ability. Conformity to His will in all things is the key to interior peace, joy, and happiness.

Peace is a gift from God. I feel peaceful only when I say, "Lord, Thy will be done." Peace is tranquillity and order, promised only to persons of good will. God's composition is perfect peace.

Yosemite Valley, California
  Painting by A. Quartuccio

NATURE

Awe of God's Creation

It is often said that the best things in life are free. The beauties and splendors of nature are there for all to see and enjoy. I can't help but wonder at the Creator of the fantastic sunrises and sunsets that I attempt to paint. All nature mirrors and witnesses the beauty, power, and perfection of Almighty God, the Divine Artist. I gain a deep appreciation of His majesty in the purity of mountain snow, the tumbling roar of waterfalls, and the restlessness of the pounding sea. The psalmist writes:

> *"The heavens declare the glory of God;*
> *the sky proclaims its builder's craft."*
> (Psalm 19:2)

God is reflected in His creation. Beauty is everywhere. Details that escape the average person catch my eye as a painter. A tiny flower among the weeds, no larger than a small button, becomes a magnificent blossom when I paint it on a large canvas for viewers to enjoy.

Catch the power of lightning flashes, or the ever changing seasons. I have observed the softly blended shades of green and brown on a grasshopper. I have strained my neck gazing at the masses of billowy white clouds after a fresh rainfall. Yes, the world speaks to me of God. This earthly beauty is only a faint reflection of what His heavenly home must be.

This realization of God's magnificent artistry and majesty came to me while camping in the barren rocky

The Milky Way — Baja nights

The psalmist writes:

*"The heavens declare the glory of God;
the sky proclaims its builder's craft."*
                          (Psalm 19:2)

desert of remote central Baja California, Mexico, as the twilight evening faded into a clear, sparkling, moonlit night.

I walked in the soft, sandy soil, illuminated by the light of a full moon which gave the landscape an eerie look. Gazing skyward, I stood in awe of it all. How beautiful were the stars! No smog or haze marred the view. The Milky Way stretched across the dome of the sky.

A soft rustling breeze broke the stillness of the night. God's presence entered my heart and my lips uttered a deep prayer of thankfulness. High above me stood the Divine artist proclaiming His glory. I, a tiny echo of His creation, stood in humble adoration. The moonlight cast long shadows across the land. Around me were the strangely-shaped Boojum Ciro cacti, which grow only in Baja. A rim of dark mountains stood over the desert. A lonesome feeling prevailed. I was totally alone — just me and my God!

Peace entered my soul as I contemplated His heavens.

SEEKING GOD

If you watch television long enough, you may come to the conclusion that mankind is very unhappy. Everyone is looking for happiness, but few find it. The media lead you to believe that happiness is gained through materialism.

The constant bombardment of the news with pictures of murder, war, famine, civil strife, the horrors of human tragedy, often casts a gloom over people's lives. Peace? Everyone wants peace, but people are looking for it in the wrong places. Peace comes from a pure heart and a love of God.

I hear Christ's words:

"Do not store up for yourselves treasures on earth, where moth and decay destroy, and thieves break in and steal. But store up treasures in heaven, where neither moth nor decay destroys, nor thieves break in and steal. For where your treasure is, there also will your heart be."

(Matt. 6:19-21)

Often man does the reverse and seeks the things of the world first, leaving God for later. Many waste their time seeking earthly pleasures alone. Many toil in the pursuit of money for its own sake. The endless search for worldly goods never ends until it consumes them. They exhaust all their energy accumulating wealth, only to have death rob them, and their lifelong work inherited by others.

The quest for gold and riches has driven many across the sea to new lands, scrambling madly for the earth's possessions. Men pan for specks of gold in mountain streams; miners dig in dark underground tunnels, braving death for the precious metals.

Explorers dive into the depths of the oceans, climb to the highest mountains, or penetrate the cold icy regions of the poles, all seeking more knowledge of the earth's secrets. Doctors probe deeper into medicine, and astronomers scan the universe, while, with the advent of new technology, man can land on the moon and further explore outer space.

What is man really looking for? I reason that beneath his search for nature's secrets he is really looking for God, the source of all knowledge. For it is He who instills in the human heart the yearning to know the truth.

In the pursuit of knowledge, many have burned their eyes out reading every book that comes across their path; the quest for learning never stops. Man seeks the whys and the wherefores of material things, to enrich his life and to be happy. But he must know that in order to live successfully, truth is the goal.

I have come to realize that earthly knowledge is necessary and important to my well-being. But knowing God and putting Him first in my life is more important than accumulating all the knowledge in all the libraries in the world.

A CRY FOR GOD

The search for God is the driving force of my life. Unless I can learn to know, serve, and love Him, life is cheap, worthless, and self-defeating. If there is no God, then why not live as I please, be my own little God, and make up my own rules? Why should I worry about others? Why be good? I should squeeze every possible pleasure out of life that I can, for tomorrow I die. Why not? If the grave is the end, then why not enjoy life while I can?

Something inside me says no. How dreadful! Is this all there is to life? Oh, no! There is hope, because God is real — a living God whose spirit rules the world. God is, always has been, and always will be.

"O God, you are my God —
  for you I long!
For you my body yearns;
  for you my soul thirsts,
Like a land parched, lifeless,
  and without water."
                    (Psalm 63:1-2)

I know by my faith that there is a God. He is a personal God with intelligence and will, who is goodness and love. I believe He is in contact with man and has revealed absolute truths about Himself.

This God put me on earth for some reason. He loves me and never fails me. It is I who sometimes fail to return that love, when I forget Him or ignore Him. No, He deserves my utmost respect.

When I break relations with Him through sin, my relations with other people also suffer. The evils of the world result because I forget God by seeking my own will instead of the Divine will.

I can't give what I don't have. If I lack peace in my soul, how can I give peace to others? How blind I am if I do not seek Him! He sees all the people who ever lived, knows every blade of grass, every flower and every grain of sand at the seashore. He is beyond time.

He knows every hair on my head and every cell in my body. Most important, He knows my secret thoughts and my intentions, and all that is on my mind before I even think it.

God knows everything! Nothing can escape Him. But I cannot see God except through faith; I must believe Him through His revelation made to man. In order to be happy here on earth and in eternity, my destiny is to do His will. I must give Him honor, praise, and glory. I must thank Him for his blessings.

O Lord, help me to know You, to know myself as I truly am, never to presume Your goodness or to take You for granted. I need to remember always, that without Thy grace, I would fail. My life would be empty, full of nothingness. Help me to see Thee, to know Thee, and to receive Thy love.

WAYS TO GOD

In all ages and in every culture, religions flourished and dominated people's lives. Self-proclaimed prophets continually come forth and announced new religions. Man needs God. Why? The answer is that God is basic to our very existence. Logic tells me that only He can provide a true religion. Because God is perfect, His religion must be perfect and contain no errors. I have studied and examined the various religions, each claiming to be the only way to worship God. I compared the founders of the major religions.

In matters of religion, I seek not the opinions and ideas of men to touch my inner soul, but the truth of God, which alone can satisfy my heart. Although there have been many sincere leaders, prophets and philosophers who founded religious movements, I find myself asking a very serious question: In whom should I place my trust, my life, my love, and allegiance to achieve the purpose for which I was born? The question is of supreme importance to me, for my eternal salvation is at stake.

When I embark upon a long and difficult journey, I do not blindly drive down any road hoping it will bring me to my destination. I study a reliable map, chart the most direct course, and faithfully follow the directions. Likewise in religion, there are many signs, each proclaiming a way of life, a philosophy, a creed, and a direction toward my destination. Even though all of them contain some basic common truth, I find many contradictions.

Some of the contradictions concern the very nature of God, such as the mystery of the Trinity. Some affirm it, others deny it. There are those who believe in re-incarnation, while others dismiss the existence of hell and even doubt that there is a heaven. In many important aspects of people's lives, such as marriage, there exist serious contradictions: One wife, one husband in commitment for life, or one man with many wives?

Searching for an answer, I combed the pages of history and found only one who stands scrutiny as the claimant to divinity, one who proved that He is God, who is sinless, and worthy of belief. I find His claim serious, for God cannot lie. That person is Jesus Christ, true God and true man, who redeemed mankind. His life, His teachings, His love and His credibility are beyond question. Everything about Jesus has been validated for me.

CHRIST, MY MODEL

Only in Christ do I find the meaning of life and solutions to the problems of human behavior. In Him I place my complete faith and the confidence of my total belief.

Who is Jesus Christ? He Himself asked that question of Peter and the apostles:

> *He said to them, "But who do you say that I am?" Simon Peter said in reply, "You are the Messiah, the Son of the living God."*
>
> (Matt. 16:15-16)

Two thousand years later the same question is being asked. Christ is the central figure in world history. His profound teachings changed the world and separated the time between B.C. and A.D. The coming of Christ into the world made the most explosive impact in the history of mankind. He turned so many people's lives and beliefs upside down. He gave a new vision of life, death, and final destiny to every human being. Christ brought a Divine message to a world suffering under the weight of slavery and sin.

What makes Him different from other great religious leaders? His followers believe that Jesus is God made man. He claimed to be God, and spoke as one having Divine authority, above kings, rulers and prophets. His mission was to redeem man, to die for our sins, and open the door to heaven to those who do His will. He demands faith and complete obedience to His word. He asks us to renounce earthly riches for the kingdom of heaven, and to willingly give up life itself in order to gain eternal life.

Jesus Christ made a stupendous claim that finally brought him to death by crucifixion. He claimed to be God. He not only made the claim, but predicted his resurrection, saying that He would rise on the third day. His rising from the tomb, his triumph from death, and his ascension to heaven created a new dawn to renew civilization. Nothing would ever be the same.

The Gospels of Matthew, Mark, Luke, and John, and the New Testament, the loftiest writings of God, record the life and deeds of Christ and revelations of the supernatural life of God come to life in Jesus Christ.

While many religious founders pointed their separate ways to God, Christ came and spoke in His own name. He proclaimed that He was the Messiah, sent by his Father to do His will. Then Christ astounded his listeners by stating that He and the Father are one; seeing Him is seeing the Father also.

He was born poor, owning nothing, yet Christ did what no mere man has ever done. In his human nature He acted as man, but in his Divine nature He acted as God. He walked on water, and stilled the wind in a storm. At the marriage feast of Cana, He changed water into wine. While preaching to thousands on a hillside, he fed them all by multiplying a few fishes and loaves of bread into many.

He cured the sick, gave sight to the blind, and healed the lepers. The dead He raised to life. He expelled demons out of possessed people. He forgave sinners and instructed them to avoid evil and to repent, to seek the kingdom of heaven first or perish.

Jesus had compassion for the poor, the victims of injustice, the oppressed, and the worst of sinners. He

*Painted from a sketch made in the Crypt of St. Cecilia.
Inspired from a visit to the Catacomb of St. Callistus in Rome.*

warned that the love of riches makes entrance to heaven very difficult. He preached humility, for the proud He resists.

Yes, Christ is my model. It is extremely important to know who He is, why He came, and what His message is. I, by the grace of God, have been blessed with the faith to believe Him. It is my hope to make Jesus known to whomever seeks Him by sharing my peace, joy, and happiness in Him.

Christ says:

*"I am the light of the world.
Whoever follows me will not walk in darkness,
but will have the light of life."*

(John 8:12)

If I follow Him, I will not walk in darkness. I must show a good example so that people can see Christ in me; thus I lead others to Him.

Actions speak louder than words. If I show a bad example, I turn people away from Christ and His Church. Perhaps I lead them to sin and the loss of their souls. Christ wants me to love all people so He can love the world through me. I am weak, however, and need His grace to accomplish this task.

I will try to give what I have received — my love, my faith in Christ and His Church, and what little knowledge I possess — to help others to know Him better.

I will help God through my deeds and day-by-day living. I will try to help bring Christ to others in an effort to heal the ills of society, and to help people learn to love God. I hope that they will achieve their spiritual destiny, which leads to heaven.

Jesus has influenced my life. He is the best example for me to follow, yet I have never met Him, seen Him, nor have I heard His voice, except through His Church and the Holy Scripture!

THANK GOD! Christ is living in the world. He is the word made flesh, God taking on a human nature in all things except sin. So, too, I can become Christ-like, a child of God, an heir to heaven. How thankful I am! A freshness of breath rests my soul. How happy is my spirit, all because Jesus loves me!

How dreadful life would be without the love of Christ! The world had been aching for a Savior because sin and darkness entered the world through the disobedience of our first parents, Adam and Eve. It was Jesus Christ, the light of the world, who came and redeemed us. The prophecies, miracles, and His resurrection from the dead are His claim to Divinity.

To know Jesus is to love Him, but many will not take the trouble to read or study Him for fear that they will have to change their lifestyles. His truths transform them. A reading of the New Testament on Christ's life, passion, and death on the cross will challenge their sense of life's meaning. But there is no in-between; one is either for Him or against Him.

Christ is my role model. People look for someone to imitate, and Jesus is the perfect model — He is God. He is Holy, believable, noble, virtuous, kind, compassionate, true, forgiving, gentle, lovable, love itself, all-knowing, with all the attributes pertaining to God. Christ is the perfect man. His spirit rules the world.

THE SERMON ON THE MOUNT

Christ gave me a new teaching to guide my life when He preached to the people on the hillside. The Sermon on the Mount stands as the greatest sermon ever preached, for it is of God.

When he saw the crowds, he went up the mountain, and after he had sat down, his disciples came to him. He began to teach them, saying:

The Beatitudes
"Blessed are the poor in spirit,
*   for theirs is the kingdom of heaven.*
Blessed are they who mourn,
*   for they will be comforted.*
Blessed are the meek,
*   for they will inherit the land.*
Blessed are they who hunger and thirst
*   for righteousness,*
*   for they will be satisfied.*
Blessed are the merciful,
*   for they will be shown mercy.*
Blessed are the clean of heart,
*   for they will see God.*
Blessed are the peacemakers,
*   for they will be called children of*
*   God.*
Blessed are they who are persecuted for
*   the sake of righteousness,*
*   for theirs is the kingdom of heaven.*
(Matt. 5:1-10)

The Church was established to guide me to obtain salvation through the teachings of Jesus Christ, my Lord and Savior.

FAITH

A Gift From God

Faith is a gift from God. I cannot earn it, demand it, nor acquire it without His grace. I did nothing to deserve faith, and it is the most precious treasure that I possess. Faith is a precious pearl, a priceless gift.

At baptism, God gave me a supernatural life of grace in my soul. In baptism, I became a child of God and was given the right to merit heaven. The faith I received while an infant must grow until my last breath, for it is here on earth that I can gain grace to enter the kingdom of God in heaven.

The faith that I received is not just any faith — it is the Catholic faith. During my youth, I began to seek answers to my questions, and even though I had faith my mind was inquisitive. I wanted more adult answers to satisfy my yearnings for the truth.

I reviewed the old questions that lingered in my mind. Who am I? What am I? What is the purpose of life? What happens after death? Why is there so much evil in the world? What is truth? The Catholic faith gives me answers to these questions. It is God-given religion which consists of truths to be believed and a life to be lived. I could never have discovered these truths by myself.

The Catholic faith is also a rational faith, because it is based on reason and common sense. Being a rational person, I know with certainty that it is true if it is not contrary to reason. To have faith means to believe what Christ has revealed. Although I cannot fully understand the mysteries of these truths, I accept them on His authority because God can neither deceive nor be deceived. God is truth and Christ says He is God. Therefore, Christ is truth, and it follows that truth is not an abstract thing — truth is a person, Christ-God!

This faith gives me strength and a worldwide vision of life that I experience within myself. Faith in Christ gives me a beautiful outlook in this world of darkness. His Spirit guides me in all things I do. Although there is no perfect happiness here on earth, faith fills the longing of my heart. The Catholic faith gives me an extra dimension, as I find in Christ the true standard of right and wrong — the true standard of morality and decency. I contrast Christ's teachings with the standards of the world. When they oppose each other, it is better to obey God than men.

The Basilica of St. Peter's in Rome.

CHRIST'S CHURCH

The only true Church of Christ is the Catholic (universal) Church, as any serious historian will discover if studying with an honest mind. It is the sole custodian of Christ's revealed truths and stands as a living witness to the authority and authenticity of the New Testament and the traditions of Christ's teachings.

Christ established one Church, not hundreds of conflicting doctrines. God is one and truth is one, and the path to salvation must be sure and true.

Our Lord did not leave me bewildered as to what I must believe and do to merit heaven. He left a Holy Society, a Church that I can recognize and to which I must belong through baptism.

He has given certain characteristic marks to identify His true Church positively: it must be ONE, HOLY, CATHOLIC (universal), and APOSTOLIC.

This Church, according to the will of Christ, is destined for people in all ages. It will endure for all time. It will teach people the truths He revealed and will provide means of holiness to members. This Church traces its origins to Christ in the lawful successors of the Apostles.

Christ gathered together twelve men, taught them, and gave them authority to carry on His work of salvation. He chose one, the Apostle Peter, to establish and be the head of His Church:

Apostle Peter
Chosen by Christ to head His Church

> *"And so I say to you, you are Peter, and upon this rock I will build my church, and the gates of the netherworld shall not prevail against it. I will give you the keys to the kingdom of heaven. Whatever you bind on earth shall be bound in heaven; and whatever you loose on earth shall be loosed in heaven."*
>
> (Matt. 16:18-19)

It was to the Apostles that Christ gave assurance that His Church would not fail, and that He would be with them until the end of time. He would send the Holy Spirit to guide the Church. To Peter, He gave His keys as head of His Church, and it is in those united with Peter that you will find the fullness of faith. For almost two thousand years the successors of Peter have been known as the Popes in the eternal city of Rome.

Before Christ ascended into heaven, He commanded His Apostles to spread His good news throughout the whole world:

> *"All power in heaven and on earth has been given to me. Go, therefore, and make disciples of all nations, baptizing them in the name of the Father, and of the Son, and of the holy Spirit, teaching them to observe all that I have commanded you. And behold, I am with you always, until the end of the age."*
>
> (Matt. 28:18-20)

In the Church He founded, Jesus Christ invites all to enter: people of all nations, the poor and the rich, kings and peasants. To the worst of sinners He promises forgiveness, compassion, and mercy. He came to save sinners, and warn the wicked of hellfire.

Members share with each other the same faith, the same doctrines, the same sacraments, and are united under a head: the successor of Saint Peter, the Pope. The central act of worship, the Eucharistic celebration, binds them together.

His revealed religion has its source in tradition and an historical book called the Bible, especially the New Testament. Christ was the expected Messiah, the Anointed One, according to the Old Testament. The Jewish nation prophesied His coming, and Christ was the fulfillment of that promise.

He came to earth to free people from sin. By His life, passion, death on the cross, and resurrection, Jesus obtained for all the chance to enter heaven. He died for all the sins of mankind.

There are many who contend that one religion is as good as another. These people may say this in all sincerity; however, I find it a contradiction. Various religions existed before Christ. Surely, there would be no need for Him to come to earth, humbling himself, enduring the horrible agony of death on the cross, unless He came to bring the true revealed message of God: to worship Him in spirit and truth.

Pope John Paul II
Successor to Saint Peter

photo courtesy of Apostolic Pro-Nuncio, Washington D.C.

Saint Paul warned about division in the early Church:

"I, then, a prisoner for the Lord, urge you to live in a manner worthy of the call you have received, with all humility and gentleness, with patience, bearing with one another through love, striving to preserve the unity of the spirit through the bond of peace: one body and one Spirit, as you were also called to the one hope of your call; one Lord, one faith, one baptism; one God and Father of all, who is over all and through all and in all."
(Ephesians 4:1-6)

Christ also warned that many false prophets would come to lead people astray, and so it has happened through the centuries. Many have broken the unity of the Church, and various religions have arisen to proclaim new revelations from God, brushing aside Christ's assurance that His Church would never fail.

My Lord places an obligation on me to listen to the Church:

"Whoever listens to you listens to me. Whoever rejects you rejects me. And whoever rejects me rejects the one who sent me."
(Luke 10:16).

I listen to the Church seriously, for to me the voice of Christ is the Catholic Church. She is an infallible guide in matters of faith and morals. She is my measuring rod of truth and my rule of faith. She speaks with the authority of Christ Himself in an unbelieving world that often ridicules Her teachings and moral standards.

Historical evidence points to the tremendous influence that Christ's teachings have had on mankind. His moral standard lifted the lives of men and women to a high degree of holiness. He transformed society and the way people should live. Through the Church's Sacraments, He gave the power for a sinner to become a saint.

Christ's divinely established Church is my guide in the realm of faith. I cannot see God directly, but when the Church speaks it is God speaking to me. Christ and His Church are inseparable, for the Church is the extension of Christ through all time.

THE CHURCH IS INDESTRUCTIBLE

The Church that Jesus Christ founded is indestructible. He promised that all the forces of evil will not destroy Her. Two thousand years of history have shown Her to be a powerful moral force in the world. The Spirit of Christ is alive, and resides deeply in the hearts of mankind. He assures us of His abiding presence:

> *"And behold, I am with you always, until the end of the age."*
>
> (Matt. 28:20)

The Holy Spirit moves the minds and wills of all who seek truth and holiness. God raises saintly people to give witness to His truth. Men and women such as Saint Augustine, Saint Thomas Aquinas, Saint Teresa of Avila, Saint Catherine of Siena, and many other Saints of the Catholic faith have defended the Church against those who would destroy Her.

All the powerful might of the Roman Empire could not subdue Her Spirit. After centuries of persecutions, heresies, enemies from within and without, from kings, dictators, freethinkers, revolutions, communism, secularism and other isms, the Catholic Church shines like a beacon of light in a world gone dark with madness.

The assaults on the Church only make Her stronger. Dark clouds always threaten Her, but the "Bark of Peter" sails safely through troubled waters. Christ predicted that those who follow Him would be persecuted for His sake. Yet, His Church has stood the test of time. No other institution in the world has had an unchangeable, continuous existence to this day. All human institutions are constantly changing, but the Catholic faith, handed down by Christ, is the same today as when He proclaimed it. It is a body of believers, a living Church, guided by the Holy Spirit.

Why is the Catholic Church so hated by its enemies? It is because it teaches Christ, true God and true man, Christ Divine. We have the choice to accept His doctrines or reject them, but the Catholic Church remains faithful to the gospel of Christ. It does not conform to the whims or novelties of the times. It will not water down Christ's eternal truths and morals to win converts.

It is not possible to change any one of the Catholic doctrines without destroying the unity that Christ had in mind. It is His Divine Authority that stands behind these truths. The teachings He proclaimed have the tremendous power to elevate a sincere soul to holiness, preparing him to meet his maker.

The Popes throughout the ages, from Saint Peter to Pope John Paul II, have been better guides to goodness and dignity than most rulers. Aside from a few worldly Popes, the overwhelming majority were saintly men who governed the Church with much more wisdom than kings, dictators, and other leaders of nations.

I have often been asked what makes me so certain that the faith I hold is true. Truth, many people say, changes with time and conditions; therefore there is no absolute truth. My answer is simple; I believe Christ before believing anyone else. Nothing in all the annals of history can compare to His claim to Divinity and Holiness, or to his lofty teachings. Faith in Him is the source of my peace, joy, and happiness.

A SUMMARY OF FAITH

From the earliest account of Christianity, the truths proclaimed by Christ were formulated in a creed called the "Apostle's Creed." It is a summary of my Catholic Faith, handed down through the centuries to the present day. How often I have repeated this creed without thinking of the meaning that it contains. But one day I recited it slowly and meditated on every word.

"I BELIEVE IN GOD..."
Yes, I firmly believe in Thee, for Thou art the Supreme Being, infinitely perfect, who made me and all things, and keeps everything in existence.

"THE FATHER ALMIGHTY..."
What a privilege to be able to call God my Father! That makes me a son. He is not a God of fear, but a loving Father.

"CREATOR OF HEAVEN AND EARTH..."
Now I know how the world and everything in it began. He created it. His stamp is on all creation if only I look for it. Nothing can come from the void, or from blind chance.

"AND IN JESUS CHRIST, HIS ONLY SON, OUR LORD..."
God sent His only begotten son, the Word made flesh, my Redeemer, who is the Savior of all mankind. By His Holiness, prophecies, miracles, and His passion, death, and resurrection, Christ proved His divinity.

Crucifix.

"WHO WAS CONCEIVED BY THE HOLY GHOST, BORN OF THE VIRGIN MARY..."

I believe that God can do anything. By the power of the Holy Spirit, Christ was conceived and became a man in the womb of the Blessed Virgin Mary.

"SUFFERED UNDER PONTIUS PILATE, WAS CRUCIFIED, DIED, AND WAS BURIED..."

I not only believe in these events marking the end of my Savior's public life, but history itself confirms this momentous happening. No one has ever suffered for me as Jesus Christ has. He carried His cross for my sins, and bore my ingratitudes, and yet promised me eternal salvation if I take up His cross and follow Him.

"HE DESCENDED INTO HELL; THE THIRD DAY HE ROSE AGAIN FROM THE DEAD..."

It is this truth that is my greatest consolation. The resurrection is proof that He is God, for only God has the power of life and death. Rising from the dead, He gives me hope that I, too, will rise with Him into everlasting life.

"HE ASCENDED INTO HEAVEN, SITTETH AT THE RIGHT HAND OF GOD, THE FATHER ALMIGHTY..."

The ascension of Christ into heaven tells me that there really is a heaven. He promises to open the gates of Paradise for His followers. He invites me, too, to seek His Kingdom here on earth, His Church, and to share the glory of eternal life in heaven.

"FROM THENCE HE SHALL COME TO JUDGE THE LIVING AND THE DEAD..."

Again, this truth consoles me, for only through faith have I seen Christ; the One whom I loved throughout the years of my life, the One whom each day I turn to and receive in Holy Communion at Mass, the One who forgives my sins. It is He whom I long to see; yes, He will be my Judge on judgment day. If I truly love Christ, then this love casts out fear; how should I fear the one I love?

"I BELIEVE IN THE HOLY GHOST..."

Christ promised to send the Holy Spirit to guide and sanctify the Church. The Holy Spirit descended upon the Apostles on Pentecost in the form of tongues of fire. The Holy Spirit is also in my heart, dwelling in me through His grace as long as I do not commit mortal sin and break my friendship with Him, for my body is His temple.

"THE HOLY CATHOLIC CHURCH..."

This one truth is a stumbling block to many, that Christ founded one Church for all to enter, one Faith, one Lord, one Baptism. Upon Peter, the first Pope, He gave the powers to teach, sanctify, and rule until the end of time. Guided by the Holy Spirit, the forces of evil will not be able to destroy it.

"THE COMMUNION OF SAINTS..."

Some do not believe in the communion of saints, but it is a beautiful doctrine to me. The Church is a family of believers. Those on earth, including me, are the Church militant, struggling against the world, the flesh, and the devil, the enemies of my soul. I still have to fight my daily battles against sin, hoping to attain heaven when God calls me home.

The Church suffering are those souls who have attained heaven, but must be purified in purgatory before entering the Holy Presence of Almighty God.

The Church triumphant in heaven are those who have attained their salvation, the Blessed ones. My father, aunts and uncles, relatives, friends, and people that I have never known, all can pray for me and I can pray to them. That is what the communion of saints means. The saints, who are in the presence of God, can intercede for me, especially Mary, my Blessed Mother.

"THE FORGIVENESS OF SINS..."

Jesus died so that my sins can be forgiven. I am grateful to Him for the Sacrament of Confession. He gave the power to His Church through ordained priests to forgive me when I fall from grace. I find the peace, joy, and happiness that our Lord promised in confession, knowing for sure that my sins are forgiven.

"THE RESURRECTION OF THE BODY..."

I know that I must die, because death is the consequence of sin. I pray daily for the grace of a happy death. Someday my body will corrupt and return to dust. I try always to be ready, by beginning the day with Mass, for I know not when death will strike like a thief in the night. I pray and hope to live each moment as if it were my last.

"AND LIFE EVERLASTING. AMEN."

With God's grace, the end of my life is the goal of my life, the reason for my existence: the Beatific Vision, the sight of the living God, and perfect and everlasting happiness in the love of my Creator.

This creed sums up what I believe, and directs all my actions in what I do. Had God not revealed these truths, I would still be in sin, in spiritual darkness, and devoid of any hope of a future life.

*On the last day, the angel's trumpet will sound the call;
then our bodies will unite with our souls,
rising from the graves. From there, all will be
in the presence of God and live forever in eternity.*

Cathedral — Monreale, Sicily
The Church of my Baptism.

MEANS OF HOLINESS

The Sacraments

I am happy that God has given me the means to attain holiness and goodness through the Sacraments of the Church. Jesus Christ instituted the Sacraments as outward signs by which grace is given to the soul. I realize that without His grace, the long road of life is almost impossible. The forces of evil, the world, the flesh, and the devil are constantly assailing me. Sin is the greatest evil to overcome, and in order to be good I need the grace of God.

It is through the Sacraments that I receive these graces. In BAPTISM, I received a new supernatural life, full of grace, and became an adopted son of God and an heir to heaven. The Sacrament cleanses away Original Sin from my soul. By the priest pouring water on my forehead and saying, *"I baptize thee in the name of the Father, and of the Son, and of the Holy Spirit,"* I became a member of God's family, the Holy Catholic Church.

I received my baptism in the beautiful Cathedral in Monreale, Sicily, Italy. Fifty years later, in 1973, I returned to see the magnificent baptismal font in the Church. There I reflected on my mother's bringing me to that place to be baptized: this was the beginning of my supernatural life of grace.

CONFIRMATION is the Sacrament whereby I received the Seal of the Holy Spirit. It makes the receiver a soldier of Christ, strengthens his faith in the face of persecution, defends it, and advances the cause of Christ to an unbelieving world. The bishop extends his hands over the person to be confirmed and prays that the Holy spirit will come down to him or her. He anoints the forehead with oil (chrism) in the form of a cross, and says: *"I sign thee with the sign of the cross and I confirm thee with the chrism of salvation, in the name of the Father, and of the Son, and of the Holy Spirit."*

   I believe that the greatest Sacrament is that of the HOLY EUCHARIST, a sacrifice and a banquet at the same time, where Christ's passion and resurrection are recalled. During the words of consecration by an ordained priest, Christ becomes present in the form of bread and wine at the Holy Sacrifice of the Mass. It is the true Body and Blood of Jesus Christ, His divinity and soul. He is contained, offered, and received.

If I should fall into sin, Christ extends forgiveness to me in the Sacrament of RECONCILIATION, or CONFESSION. Through the power He gave to the priest:

> *"Receive the holy Spirit. Whose sins you forgive are forgiven them, and whose sins you retain are retained."*
>
> (John 20:22-23)

He re-instates me in His loving grace and mercy. The consolation that comes from confession is a source of peace, joy, and happiness that money cannot buy.

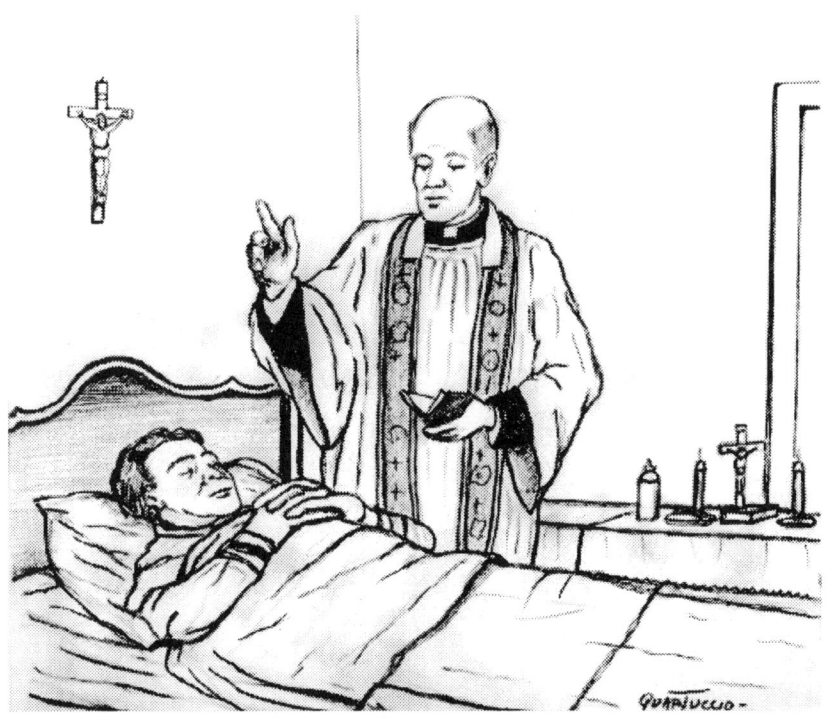

When illness strikes and death is near, the Church administers the Sacrament of the ANOINTING OF THE SICK. The body breaks down. It is attacked by disease, accident, and old age. When in danger of death, the Sacrament strengthens and comforts the soul and prepares it for the final hours of life. The priest will anoint me with Holy Oils accompanied by prayers to help restore my health or to prepare me to meet my God.

Saint James in the Gospel says:

"Is anyone among you sick? He should summon the presbyters of the church, and they should pray over him and anoint [him] with oil in the name of the Lord, and the prayer of faith will save the sick person, and the Lord will raise him up. If he has committed any sins, he will be forgiven."
(James 5:14-15)

HOLY ORDERS is the Sacrament whereby bishops, priests, and other ministers are ordained. They receive the power and grace given by Christ to carry on their sacred Church duties. I have attended many solemn ordination ceremonies of friends who have answered the call to the priesthood, that long line of men chosen by Christ to perpetuate the sacrifice of the Mass. At the Last Supper, Jesus said:

> *"Do this in memory of me."*
> (Luke 22:19)

Another gift is the grace that comes from the Sacrament of MATRIMONY. I have committed myself to Christ in a Christian marriage to a woman for life until death. It is He who was the invisible witness, the third partner. Here, again, I have the joy of knowing that God, my Lord Jesus Christ, is with me and my wife throughout our married life if we cooperate with the grace given in this Sacrament. The fact that God elevated marriage to a Sacrament gives me comfort; I know that He is beside me when hard times come to the two of us. The ring on my finger means something to me, for a vow is a serious commitment.

> *"So they are no longer two, but one flesh. Therefore, what God has joined together, no human being must separate."*
>
> (Matt. 19:6)

IN TOUCH WITH GOD

The Mass

At the Last Supper, Christ instituted the Eucharistic Sacrifice and celebrated the first Mass. This is one of the most momentous events in the history of mankind, for at this banquet Jesus gave Himself to us in Holy Communion:

> *"While they were eating, Jesus took bread, said the blessing, broke it, and giving it to his disciples said, `Take and eat; this is my body.' Then he took a cup, gave thanks, and gave it to them, saying, 'Drink from it, all of you, for this is my blood of the covenant, which will be shed on behalf of many for the forgiveness of sins.' "*
>
> (Matt. 26:26-28).

Christ commanded His apostles to do this in commemoration of Him as a last will and testament. He authorized them also to change bread and wine into His Body and Blood. Christ offered Himself to God in an unbloody and sacramental manner, so the work of our redemption is continued at every Mass. For two thousand years, the Holy Sacrifice of the Mass has been offered throughout the world in the same unbloody manner, bringing the Lord, in the form of bread and wine, to His people on earth as He did at the Last Supper. The Mass is the center of my Christian life, for it is a true sacrifice.

At the last supper, Christ gave us the Holy Eucharist
— The Mass —

The Last Supper —Painting in the Church of the Nativity, Basilica, Bethlehem

When the priest elevates the Host and Chalice after the consecration, he pronounces Christ's words: *"This is My Body"* and *"This is My Blood."* At that moment I gaze at Christ, at God, and see Him — *"My Lord and My God!"*

I adore Him, praise Him, thank Him, give Him honor and glory, and ask Him for my daily needs.

A perfect way to begin the day is to attend Mass and offer myself to Him. I depend on Him for every spiritual and material good. In the Mass Christ is with me; being united with Him puts me in touch with God. Here I see my creator coming to me personally in Holy Communion, the food of my soul.

Father James Henry at St. Rose Church, Paso Robles, Calif.

RECEIVING CHRIST

Holy Communion

My greatest joy is approaching the altar at Mass to receive Christ in Holy Communion in prayerful awareness of His real presence. I receive not a symbolic presence, but Jesus Christ Himself. Union with God my Creator is the supreme gift that Christ promised at the Last Supper:

"Take and eat; this is my body."
(Matt. 26:26)

Christ meant what He said when He declared:

"I am the living bread that came down from heaven; whoever eats this bread will live forever; and the bread that I will give is my flesh for the life of the world."
(John 6:51)

There is no gift as precious as God's own Divine life. How fortunate I am to have God come to me in the bread of life. How wonderful Christ is! How pure is his love! No mere words can express my thankfulness to Him. Contained in the white host is His love for me. No earthly king, no billionaire, neither material reward nor all the wealth in the universe can compare to one Holy Communion.

THIS IS THE ULTIMATE IN MY PEACE, JOY, AND HAPPINESS.

"Take and eat; this is my body."
(Matt. 26:26)

A DAY OF HAPPINESS

Memory of My First Communion

"To God, the joy of my youth." When I hear these words, my thoughts go back to my first Communion more than fifty years ago in Cleveland, Ohio.

During the long cold winter of 1936, two Catholic sisters came to our house on Force Avenue, asking if there were any Catholics living there. My mother answered that, being new immigrants from Italy, we were not close to the Church at present. Finding that my brother and I had not yet received our first Communion, the sisters enlisted us in the catechism class which met on Sunday after Mass at the Holy Name Church.

I was thirteen years old, and had yet to receive Christ. I owe a great debt to those two sisters, for it was their dedication and love of Jesus which were instrumental in my learning of Christ and His Church. The sister, Albertus, I believe, taught me well. Although I barely spoke English, she lovingly and patiently took the time to explain the lessons to me.

She stressed our Lord in the Holy Eucharist, the Mass, and the Commandments. Her deep faith in the Holy Communion communicated to me a tremendous love of Christ. She explained that the little white host given in Holy Communion is Our Lord, Jesus, who would come and dwell in me. My body is the temple of the Holy Spirit, and Sanctifying Grace will make my soul beautiful and pleasing to God.

I was a small, frail, simple Italian boy experiencing the inspiration of her teachings. I came to believe, and eagerly wanted to receive Jesus. Then in April of that year, after two months of instruction, my father informed the family that we were moving to San Jose, California, where the land and climate resembled Italy.

It was during the Great Depression, and jobs were scarce. My father had been out of work and our family was struggling to keep body and soul together. A cousin in California convinced him that there was work for him in the fruit orchards and canneries. Besides, in the sunny California climate he could grow all kinds of fruits and vegetables. It sounded too good to be true.

I was to make my first Communion in May, but I would miss it if we left. I was worried and spoke to the pastor and the sister who taught me. Time was short, as we were leaving on May 1st. The pastor informed my brother and me that we could make our first Communion in California. I felt unsure, as my parents might be too busy getting settled to follow up on Communion.

On April 30th, the day before the move to California, I went to say good-bye to the Fathers and Sisters of Holy Name Church. I told sister, "I would like to receive Jesus now, before I make the long trip to a strange new land." She took me to Father and explained my desire and anxiety. Father replied that I would have to make my first confession. Also, a fast was required before receiving Communion.

I said to Father: "We did fast; Joe and I haven't eaten since yesterday, and we are ready. We want to make our first Communion now." Sister agreed that we were both prepared and should receive our Lord; the priest took me into the confessional and heard my first confession. I do not recall Father's name, but I will always remember his kindness. What followed was one of the most meaningful events in my life. I will never forget that wonderful hour as long as I live.

Here I was, only thirteen years old, penniless and dressed in patched trousers, about to receive Jesus for the first time. I expected to receive Him quietly and go straight home. Instead, I was ushered with my brother down the long aisle of Holy Name Church.

To my surprise, all the sisters of the school, and several priests were in attendance to see us receive Holy Communion. As I walked down the center aisle towards the altar, the huge organ boomed out the hymn, "O Mother Dear O Pray for Me." It filled the church with heavenly music. I felt a chill run down my spine. I was in another world as I walked with folded hands toward the priest who stood below the large crucifix in the magnificent sanctuary. Holding the Host before me as I kneeled, he proclaimed *"The Body of Christ."*

"Amen," I replied. In humble adoration, I received Jesus for the first time. I felt so innocent and pure.

A glow of holiness prevailed after I received my Lord. I was in ecstasy! My brother followed me back to the pew, and I said my thanksgiving. Joe and I, two little boys, had this magnificent church all to ourselves. What an honor it was to be treated in such a special manner. In receiving Jesus, the bread from heaven, I experienced a love, a peace, a sense of holiness, a feeling hard to express.

"The Body of Christ."

After it was all over, the sisters congratulated us, and Father took Joe and me to the rectory, where a big breakfast was prepared for us. Never had we had such a feast. How good has God been to us, a heavenly banquet in the bread of life in Holy Communion, and an earthly banquet in the priest's house during the depression. Father gave each of us two dollars; a large sum in those days.

Their deep love and interest gave me a feeling of God looking down on my tender soul, and showering His grace on my first Communion day. Father gave me some encouragement: always to be faithful to God, to love Jesus, to be good and keep the commandments, and to re-enforce my faith by going to Mass and Communion.

Reaching for a drawer in his desk, he took a prayer book kit with a rosary and a scapular, and handed them to me. Father then bade both of us a hugging good-bye. Truly, peace, joy, and happiness shone down on me that day.

The example of the Church, the priests, and the sisters had a lasting influence on my whole life. Many times I recall the impact of first Communion. When I am low in spirit, the remembrance of that day, the love that flowed over me, the Church, the priests, the sisters, and the saintly sister who brought me the knowledge of my Lord and my God, all serve to remind me that God is with me. I hope that with the grace of God, I can follow in their footsteps and lead others to Christ.

NEVER ALONE

The Blessed Sacrament

In moments of sorrow, loneliness, and rejection, when the chill pressures of a loveless world crush my soul, a little voice within me lifts up my spirit. Perhaps it is my guardian angel whispering to me: "Remember, if no one seems to love you, and you feel alone, DON'T DESPAIR! God loves you — Christ loves you. Christ wants you in His loving arms, now and for eternity."

When my heart is troubled, in pain, and I seek consolation, I walk to my parish Church or to any Catholic Church that is open. I look for the lighted sanctuary lamp above the altar, indicating that Christ is present in the Blessed Sacrament. There He is waiting for me to pour out my love for Him, to empty myself, and to lay before Him all my problems.

"Lord, I tried everything. I broke my arm, my wife died after an operation, my bank account is depleted, bills are piling up, and the washing machine won't run. My old station wagon needs repairing, and my children are growing restless. Please give me Thy grace and guide me."

Then I remember His words:

"Come to me, all you who labor and are burdened, and I will give you rest. Take my yoke upon you, and learn from me, for I am meek and humble of heart; and you will find rest for yourselves. For my yoke is easy, and my burden light."
(Matt. 11:28-30)

How wonderful it is to know that the God of heaven and earth dwells in the tabernacle! What a love Christ gives me by coming to earth in a tiny host and inviting me to adore Him! Christ is in every Catholic Church in the world. What a privilege to visit the living God on the altar! Whether I am dressed in rags or purple robes, He looks on me with love and blessing.

There are many who make tremendous sacrifices to visit famous personages. Men and women seek audience with a movie star, a rock music celebrity, a sports giant, a king or queen, or great rulers of nations. Yet, what could be more blessed than to be with the King of Kings, God Himself, the Lord, Jesus in the Blessed Sacrament!

I thank God for the faith to believe what I cannot see with by bodily eyes, for I know He is there. During the many years of sorrow and hardship when I became a widower, Christ was my constant companion in the Blessed Sacrament, for He never failed me. Yes, Jesus is a living presence in the world today.

Saint Thomas the Apostle, doubted Christ's resurrection, and wanted to put his finger in Christ's wound in order to believe. Jesus said to him:

"Have you come to believe because you have seen me? Blessed are they who have not seen and have believed."

(John 20:29)

MY GUARDIAN ANGEL

Many do not believe in angels, especially guardian angels, but I do. I try to keep a personal relationship with my unseen spirit. In my heart Christ assures me that I have such a guardian to help and support me in the trials of life and on my journey to heaven. I ask my angel daily to guard me from evil and to watch over me in my work, travels, and other events of the day. Although I cannot see my angel (because it is a pure spirit without a body), it is as real to me as I am real. I take comfort in Christ's word that He has assigned to me a guardian to whom I can pray, who will be my companion throughout life.

As angels see the face of God, so I am in contact by prayer to one who is in God's presence. I read in Holy Scripture Christ's warning on giving harm to children:

> *"See that you do not despise one of these little ones, for I say to you that their angels in heaven always look upon the face of my heavenly Father."*
> (Matt. 18:10)

Thus it is in life: you are what you believe. What I believe gives me peace in my mind. Someday in heaven I will meet this angel in whom I confide and pray, and I will thank him for all eternity.

THE SAINTS

God wills my sanctification:

"So be perfect, just as your heavenly Father is perfect."

(Matt. 5:48)

He is calling me to holiness, to be a saint, to love God with my heart, mind, and soul, with everything that I have. What a challenge! It frightens me to contemplate the thought of striving to become one.

Fortunately, many before me have followed Christ and set good examples. They were men and women who lived Christlike lives and became saints. They forgot themselves, and devoted all their power of mind, body, and soul to worshipping Him and promoting His Honor, and Glory. They were full of praise for Almighty God. Finding peace in their souls, they were noble in character, cheerful, and joyful.

They found true peace, something men and women seek but seldom find in their worldly pursuits. The saints had tremendous love of God in their hearts and lives and extended that love to others in spite of hardships, suffering, and obstacles. They are a witness to God's Holiness in the mastery of their lives, conforming to the will of Christ, His Church, and His heavenly Father.

In searching for the secret of their sanctity, I discovered that they had a great love of the Mass, Communion, and the Church. The Eucharist Christ in Holy Communion worked miracles and transformed their lives.

Saint Francis was a peacemaker. He knew that true peace comes from God, and that he could not give peace to others unless he reformed himself first. By prayer and penance, by his obedience to the Holy Church and his detachment from material things, Francis became one of the greatest of Saints.

He was humble, embraced poverty, and lived simply. His dependence on God's providence, his trust, and his tremendous love for Christ were so great that they brought forth on his body the five wounds of Jesus, known as the stigmata.

Saint Francis was happy, full of joy, and he was an especially peaceful man. He loved everybody because he loved God. Money meant nothing to him — only God mattered — and eternal life was his real goal. He is the saint everyone loves. Saint Francis has influenced my life and I follow his spirit through the Secular Order of Franciscans.

People are looking for role models, but the materialistic world overlooks the saints. Instead, the glamorous giants of sports, movies, entertainment, and a host of famous personalities attract attention, even if they lead a life of scandal. Their sins are often excused by the multitudes who do not believe it is possible to become a saint in this modern world.

Prayer of Saint Francis of Assisi

Lord, make me an instrument of your peace.
Where there is hatred, let me sow love,
Where there is injury, pardon;
Where there is doubt, faith;
Where there is despair, hope;
Where there is darkness, light;
Where there is sadness, joy.

O Divine Master,
Grant that I may not so much seek:
 to be consoled as to console;
 to be understood as to understand;
 to be loved as to love;
For it is in giving, that we receive;
It is in pardoning,
 that we are pardoned;
It is in dying,
 that we are born
 to eternal
 life.

Calligraphy by John Adams

SAINT FRANCIS OF ASSISI

Peace with God • Peace with himself
Peace with nature
Peace with the world around him

I find the lives and virtues of the saints to be superior to those lives featured in the secular press and on television. Reading about the lives of Saint Ignatius of Loyola, Saint Thomas Aquinas, Saint Thomas More, Saint Catherine of Siena, or the thousands of saintly people in the history of the Catholic Church, as seen through the eyes of faith, gives me great joy.

Such great souls inspire me to imitate their virtuous examples. Knowing how they lived, learning what they did, and seeing how they acted, makes me admire them. The virtue they practiced and the shining holiness of their lives gives me hope that I, too, by the grace of God, can attain the peace, joy, and happiness that was theirs by following Christ and serving Him.

Christ filled the hearts of the saints with love. They listened to His Church, for to them following the Church was following Jesus. He established one Church and it is through this Church that they learned of Him. The power of God's grace influenced all they did through their tremendous faith. Holy Communion was their reality. The bread and wine they accepted were the Body and Blood of Christ.

Here then is the source of the saint's strength, the one great gift of God to nourish them in the struggles of life: Christ in our midst daily. The saints knew that the Eucharist is food for their souls on the journey to heaven, where Christ is waiting for them in eternal life.

What was I doing with my life? Should I waste my time and effort to pursue the secular view of life only? Thinking over the Faith I was given freely by God's grace, I realized I must not let it die. I could lose it by sin and neglect.

No, Christ's passion and death on the cross, His resurrection and triumph over sin and death, will mean nothing if I do not accept His love and return it. In spite of my weakness and sin I know God has great plans for me. I must heed His call to become a saint.

One example of a heroic follower of Christ is Father Damien De Veuster. Born in Tremeloo, Belgium in 1840, he went to the Hawaiian Islands as a missionary priest. While serving the Catholic faithful there, he saw the plight of the dreadful lepers who were exiled to the island of Molokai and treated as outcasts of society.

Father Damien, leaving the pleasures of the world to follow Christ and administer to the unloved victims of leprosy, made a tremendous impact on me. At a time when I needed to grow in my faith I asked myself, why would one give up life, marriage, money and fame to go to such a horrible place of wretched humanity unless he had a great faith in God. I saw the power of the Catholic religion in his apostolic work among those unfortunate people.

Reading of his life and work transformed me into a better Catholic. Father Damien proved to me that the road to sanctity is one of dedication, sacrifice, and a total commitment to God. He had faith in the Church's Sacraments, Mass, Communion, Confession; he believed

FATHER DAMIEN DE VEUSTER
-1840 - 1889-

The Apostle of the Lepers

Molokai Island, Hawaii

Father Damien was born in Belgium in 1840 and spent his life caring for the despised lepers on Molokai, Hawaii.

He brought faith and hope to the most wretched and unwanted lepers. He brought also attention of their plight to the world. Father Damien administered the spiritual and temporal needs of these people. Most of all, he gave the love of Christ to them. Stricken by the dreaded disease himself the beloved priest died of it in 1889.

St. Philomena Church - Built by Fr. Damien

Anthony Quartuccio

the Church would bring hope instead of despair to the lepers. Although their bodies were disfigured and ugly with the disease, Father Damien showed them that their souls were beautiful, holy, and loved by God.

An example of saintly life in our modern times is Mother Teresa of Calcutta, India. This unselfish nun founded an order of sisters dedicated to relieve the suffering and misery of poor people dying in the city streets. She fed, clothed and comforted them, and gave them a decent burial. Like Father Damien, she extended the love of Christ to the most needy of God's children.

I am convinced that if I follow My Lord Jesus Christ, obey His commandments, and listen to His Church, I will receive His grace to be a saint.

> Saint John did it.
> Saint Peter did it.
> Saint Paul did it.
> Saint Francis of Assisi did it.
> Saint Anthony did it.
> Saint Augustine did it.
> Saint Monica did it.
> Saint Rose did it.
> Saint John Bosco did it.
> Saint Vincent DePaul did it.
> Saint Francis Xavier did it.
> Saint John Mary Vianney did it.
> Saint Peter Claver did it.

And most of all the Blessed Mother Mary and Saint Joseph are my greatest hope in leading me to the love of Christ.

Reading the lives of the saints gives one the most inspiring friends. Thousands have shown the way by obeying our Lord's command to take up His cross and follow Him. In doing so, the saints gained the eternal life that He promised.

Saint Monica, mother of Saint Augustine, prayed for many years for her wayward son. Her faith was rewarded when he returned and converted to the Catholic faith and became the great Bishop Saint.

Saint Monica, mother of Saint Augustine.

PRAYER AND MEDITATION

"The Little Chapel"

Prayer is necessary to be in touch with God. In this accelerated modern world, constant activity can cause physical and mental drain; it's important to slow down. So I withdraw a few minutes each day to reflect in peace.

My Lord Jesus gives me guidance on how to pray:

"But when you pray, go to your inner room, close the door, and pray to your Father in secret. And your Father, who sees in secret will repay you."
(Matt. 6:6)

I built a "Little Chapel" within my house. It is a sacred sanctuary where I can enter quietly to pray and to rest my soul. Here I meditate and find peace with God. My home is Christ's home where He is welcomed. Should He walk through the door or come in Spirit, He would recognize the crucifix, the sacrifice of His dying on the cross for my sins. In this tiny chapel, He is honored and displayed openly, with Mary and Joseph at His side. This chapel is a miniature church with visual reminders of the Catholic faith. I constructed the large crucifix many years ago when I could not afford to buy one.

By meditating beneath this cross I learned the price Christ paid for my redemption and salvation. Each morning I greet Him in prayer, express my love for Him, and offer up my work, joy and suffering for the day to come.

Each night as I kneel at the cross, I lay my problems at His feet and examine my conscience. If I have offended our Lord or my neighbor, I ask for forgiveness. Most of all, I thank Him for His blessings and express my gratitude for the gifts of faith and my own life.

A reading from sacred scripture, or recitation of the rosary or the little office of the Franciscan Secular Order completes my expression of love for God. A vigil light glows, symbolizing Christ as the Light of the world. Dipping my fingers in the Holy Water font, I make the sign of the cross on my forehead, heart and shoulders and go to bed in peace.

GUIDE TO TRUE HAPPINESS

People tell me that the Ten Commandments are out of date, irrelevant in the complexity life of the modern world. Each person, as if enlightened, makes up his own rules of conduct as the situation arises.

No, God has given me rules, confirmed by Christ, to guide my life toward true happiness. They are a positive course of action to be followed. When He gave Moses the commandments in the old law, He required strict obedience and observance of them. Christ made it a condition for salvation:

"If you wish to enter into life, keep the commandments."
(Matt. 19:17)

When my Lord says that if I truly love Him, I must keep His commandments, I take Him seriously. God's rules set me free, for as long as I obey them, my soul is in tune with His will, and peace, joy, and happiness will surely follow.

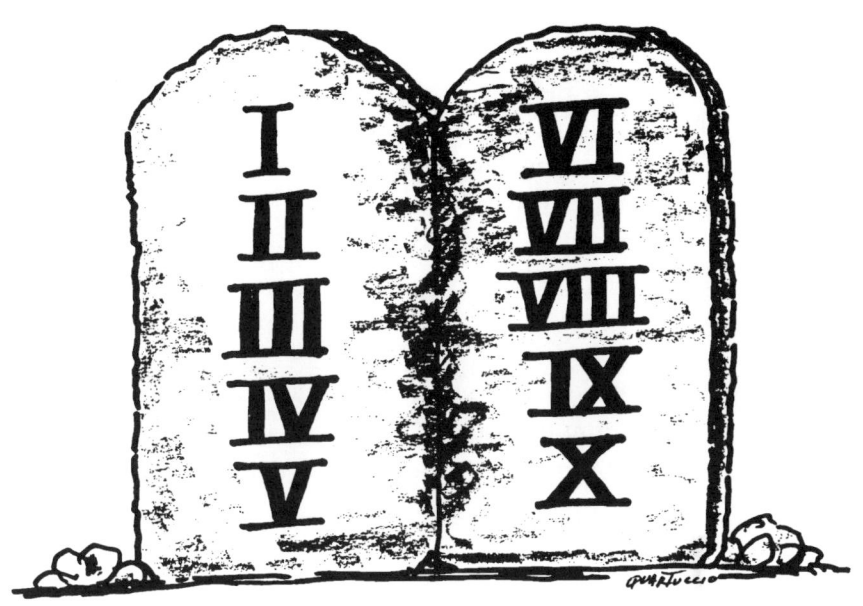

THE TEN COMMANDMENTS OF GOD

1. *I am the Lord thy God. Thou shalt not have strange gods before me.*
2. *Thou shalt not take the name of the Lord thy God in vain.*
3. *Remember thou keep holy the Lord's day.*
4. *Honor thy father and thy mother.*
5. *Thou shalt not kill.*
6. *Thou shalt not commit adultery.*
7. *Thou shalt not steal.*
8. *Thou shalt not bear false witness against thy neighbor.*
9. *Thou shalt not covet thy neighbor's wife.*
10. *Thou shalt not covet thy neighbor's goods.*

ATTAINING HAPPINESS

In the spiritual life, I cannot stand still. Either I grow, or I slip behind. I try to set a pattern for myself, realizing that I need to constantly rededicate my will to do my best and to go forward. I want to take a positive approach to daily living, and keep before me some course of action to follow.

- Upon awakening, my first thought is to bid good morning to God.
- Say the Morning Offering prayer, dedicate the day to Jesus, and my intentions to His Sacred Heart.
- If possible, I would attend Mass and receive Christ in Holy Communion.
- Remember the one purpose of life, salvation, and keep my eyes raised from the earth to heaven.
- Be at peace with God, seeking and performing His will as best I can.
- Make good use of my time, and use God's grace to avoid sin.
- Have a clear, clean, and honest conscience, living in the presence of God, dwelling in sanctifying grace.
- Always say grace before meals.
- Do my best in whatever I do at work, play, or other activities of the day.
- Develop a spirit of kindness, and treat all people as if they were Christ Himself, with love and respect.
- Do some penance or good deed.

— Offer prayers or say the rosary.
— Do some spiritual reading, and try to deepen my faith
— Avoid rash judgment.
— Forgive others and ask forgiveness for myself.
— Strive to spread peace, joy, and happiness to everyone I meet.
— Make a point to detach myself from, and not be allured by, worldly goods.
— Realize what eternity is and prepare to die daily, for life is short.
— Live in constant remembrance of the judgment, for nothing will remain hidden before God.
— Finally, upon retiring, say my nightly prayer, examine my conscience, and thank God for all His grace and blessings.

I always want to do more for God. I try to be myself, looking at every opportunity to serve Him and my fellow man. Being human, I do not always succeed, but I keep trying.

The only things that matter are having a good and true conscience, walking toward God in the state of grace, doing His will, and keeping His commandment of love. His Kingdom is within me so I am never far from home. I rejoice in the knowledge of His love for me, and the certitude of His divine providence. This gives me the strength to face my daily battles. ONLY SIN can destroy my destiny, with death as the result. With his grace I am able to see through the darkness of life's highway with a high beam light.

A STRING OF BEADS

It is fashionable in this age to discard old devotional practices such as the time-honored rosary. I find praying the rosary a beautiful expression of faith, for in the recitation of the prayers and the meditation on the life of Christ, I am mindful of the joys, sorrows, and glories of my Lord. I walk with Mary, our blessed Mother, and feel the pains of Jesus in the agony in the garden.

I recall the many scenes of Christ's life unfolding with each decade of the rosary. From His birth to the ascension to heaven, the string of beads is like a few pages from Holy Scripture. The rosary, with its mysteries of Jesus and His plan for redemption, is like a Bible in miniature.

I use my imagination to relive those biblical days as if I were present two thousand years ago. It makes me appreciate the sacrifices Jesus endured for me. The rosary is a very powerful prayer, and will bring much grace if prayed with reverence and devotion.

I pray in this form to praise God, the Virgin Mary, and our Savior and Lord, Jesus Christ.

The Hail Mary is a beautiful prayer. Mary, a virgin, was highly favored by God. The angel Gabriel announced that all generations shall call her blessed. Through her acceptance of God's will, she gave birth to our Savior, Lord Jesus Christ, who is God.

*Hail Mary, full of grace,
the Lord is with you;
blessed are you among women,
and blessed is the fruit of your womb, Jesus.
Holy Mary, Mother of God,
pray for us sinners,
now and at the hour of our death.
Amen.*

Her role in redemption is to lead us to Jesus. My devotion to her is bound up with the birth, life, death and resurrection of her Divine Son. When Jesus was dying on the cross, He gave Mary to us as our mother:

"Behold, your mother."
(John 19:27)

The rosary is my way of keeping in mind the tremendous gift of Jesus through Mary, mother of God and the Church, for without her consent, I would still be waiting for the redeemer.

DEATH

Not many people meditate on death until a serious crisis touches their lives. During World War II I was in the army medical corps, attending wounded soldiers. In military hospitals I witnessed the shattered lives of many young men and women.

I was only nineteen years old and full of life, and suddenly the war taught me that death was a real possibility. In war, the young die as well as the old. Death was always in my mind, and I didn't know what the morrow would bring.

Daily newspapers told of death and terrible destruction. The pictures of sinking ships at sea and infantry-men with rifles and bayonets charging over muddy trenches made me realize the horror of war. Planes blasted out of the sky sent shivers down my spine as I mentally placed myself with the crew.

Many of my friends never made it home. A classmate of mine was lost at sea during a bombing mission. Fortunately I was spared much of the agony of war by taking care of the wounded at home.

One night in my barracks I picked up a copy of the New Testament and read all the Gospels straight through without stopping. It had an illuminating impact on me.

Station of the Cross
St. Paulskirche in Munich, Germany

The most horrible death was endured by Jesus Christ in crucifixion. His passion and suffering made a deep impression on me. By His death and resurrection, the message was clear: life does not end at the grave — death is only the beginning of the real life beyond.

I realized that no matter how successful I am in this life, death will rob me of all earthly possessions. This revelation resulted in an oil painting I did while taking an art class after duty in San Francisco's Chinatown. A skull and a mandolin were the subjects by which I symbolized the parting of man and his prized possessions. The instrument was left behind at death, but no sound poured forth.

I began to think about my own death and how short my time really is in the light of eternity. I came face to face with the truths that Christ taught about death. My world will pass away, and then what? I was born, am living now, and each second, each minute, each hour, each day, each year, my time is drawing closer to that end.

I was born to die. Christ gives me hope, for He conquered death. In His words:

"I am the resurrection and the life; whoever believes in me, even if he dies, will live, and everyone who lives and believes in me will never die."
(John 11:25-26)

As old age advances on me, I know I must leave all worldly possessions behind; only love, goodness, and doing the will of God will follow me. The thought of parting from this world keeps me humble, for without Him I am nothing.

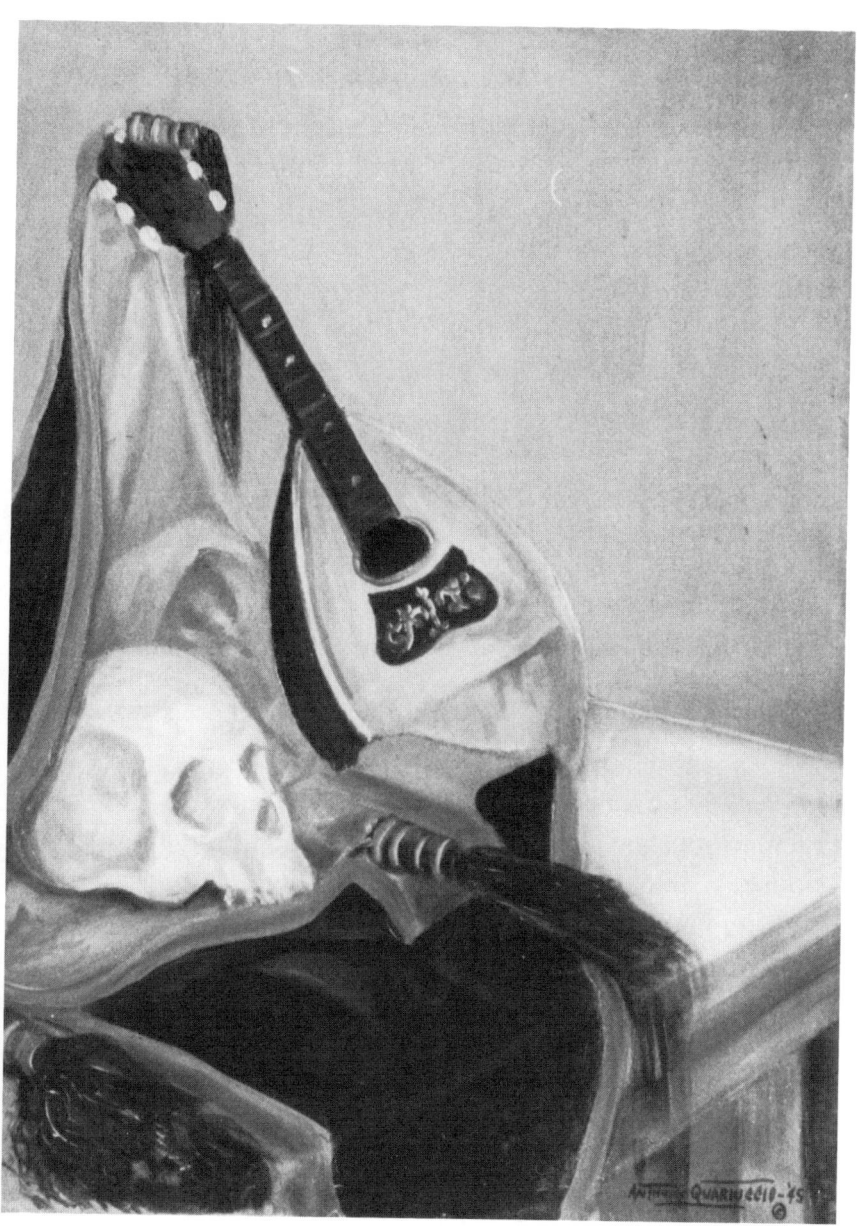

There are those who spend a lifetime putting off the terrible thought of DEATH. The uncertainty of the unknown disturbs their peace of mind and happiness, for death seems final to them. To a Catholic, life is a love affair with Christ. Death is but the doorway from the womb of the earth to the life of eternal glory, heaven.

Who isn't in fear of the unknown or terrified of utter nothingness after a brief experience of life? If the grave is the end, what a mockery! What despair! What cruelty! But God's love is all powerful. Through Christ, death is defeated. By His power I will rise again from the grave. Then He will also be my judge. If I truly love Him and am His friend, I will then rest in His love.

But with Jesus Christ's promise, O death, where is Thy sting? In His Easter resurrection is my hope. What a glorious reason for living a good and holy life here on earth for this tiny fraction of time. No, the life span that God has given me must be a precious gift for me to carefully nourish. With His love I shall strive to be perfect as the heavenly Father is perfect.

I pray daily for the grace of a happy death or whatever is His will. Many of my close friends and relatives have gone to their eternal reward. A cemetery is across from my hillside home in Paso Robles, California. Beneath a tall tree on a grassy lawn is my plot, where I too will someday find my final resting place.

On my mind is the thought of the four last things, DEATH, JUDGMENT, HELL, and HEAVEN, for I recall Christ's words:

> *"What profit would there be for one to gain the whole world and forfeit his life? Or what can one give in exchange for his life?"*
>
> (Matt. 16:26)

Death: I know death is a certainty; there is no escape, life should be a preparation for entrance to heaven.

Judgment: I have no excuses, no alibis; I know where I stand, and my life will either confirm or condemn me, for as I sow so shall I reap, says the Lord. I pray that I will persevere.

Hell: Hell is emptiness, pain, remorse, darkness, loneliness, eternal damnation; the hopelessness of ever seeing God in the Beatific Vision.

Heaven: Heaven is eternal peace, joy, happiness! Life everlasting! Here I hope to see God face to face as He is forever. This would be the fulfillment of my life.

In meditating on these four notions, I stay focused on the purpose of my life: to hate sin, and to love my neighbor and God with all my heart and soul.

WHO IS MY NEIGHBOR?

On Judgment Day I will be alone before Almighty God, hoping for a merciful judgment on the choices that I made during my lifetime. My life and my works, for good or evil, will be written in the book of life. The real test of Christian charity or love is in deeds done, not just words.

The followers of Christ are to live the faith, for without good works faith is dead. In the Gospel of Luke (6:46) I found Christ saying, *"Why do you call me, 'Lord, Lord,' but not do what I command?"*

In stronger words, He says, *"Not everyone who says to me, 'Lord, Lord,' will enter the kingdom of heaven, but only the one who does the will of my Father in heaven."*
(Matt. 7:21)

It is a challenge to live a Christ-like life. Jesus wants me to love my neighbor as myself. Who is my neighbor? All people. The whole world is my neighborhood, yet my real world is the small area where I live. I find that in reality my tiny world radiates from my house to my neighborhood, my city, my parish and nearby communities.

Of billions of people on earth, I come in contact with perhaps fifty to a hundred, not more than a thousand. Without intending neglect for those in distant lands, I feel my immediate neighbors are those I meet daily at home, at Church, in the park, at the market, and at the many other places I go.

My first charity is to love God, my wife, my children, my extended family, the parish, and then on to others. It matters little if I help those whom I cannot see and neglect those close to me, for charity begins at home.

I think often about the ultimate test of saving my soul. Being human and weak, I sometimes fail in my striving for sanctity. I attempt to do my best with purity of intention. But I realize that piety alone is not enough if it is not transformed into good works. How I treat others is the measure of how I treat Christ.

Deep in my conscience is Jesus speaking on the Last Judgment in the Gospel of Saint Matthew. I read and re-read this powerful passage:

> *"When the Son of Man comes in his glory, and all the angels with him, he will sit upon his glorious throne, and all the nations will be assembled before him. And he will separate them one from another, as a shepherd separates the sheep from the goats. He will place the sheep on his right and the goats on his left.*
>
> *Then the king will say to those on his right, 'Come, you who are blessed by my Father. Inherit the kingdom prepared for you from the foundation of the world. For I was hungry and you gave me food, I was thirsty and you gave me drink, a stranger and you welcomed me, naked and you clothed me, ill and you cared for me, in prison and you visited me.' Then the righteous will answer him and say, 'Lord, when did we see you hungry and feed you, or thirsty and give you drink? When did we see you a stranger and welcome you, or naked and clothe you? When did we see you ill or in prison, and visit you? And the king will say to them in reply, 'Amen, I say to you, whatever you did for one of these least brothers of mine, you did for me.'*

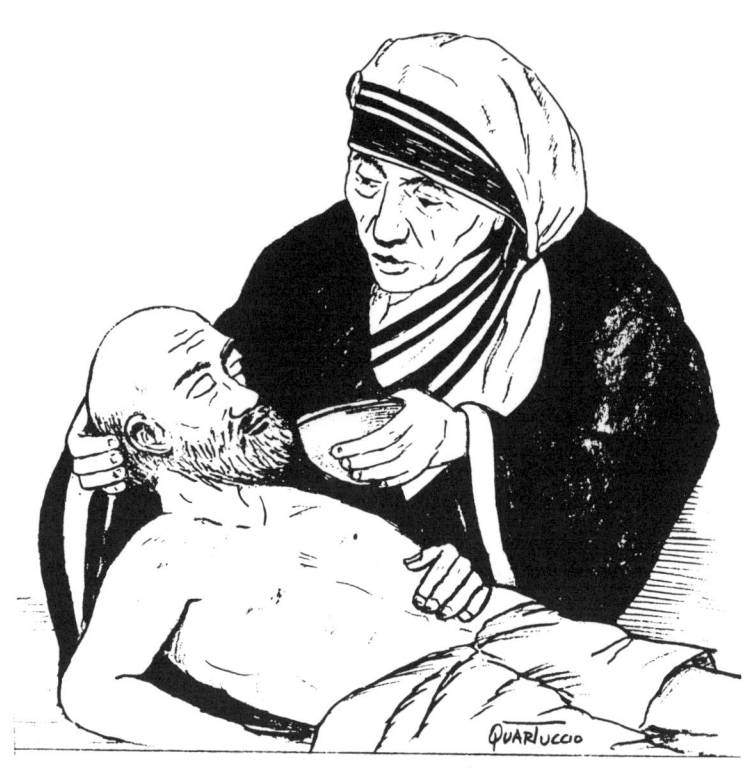

Mother Teresa comforts the poor in Calcutta, India.

Then he will say to those on his left, 'Depart from me, you accursed, into the eternal fire prepared for the devil and his angels. For I was hungry and you gave me no food, I was thirsty and you gave me no drink, a stranger and you gave me no welcome, naked and you gave me no clothing, ill and in prison, and you did not care for me.' Then they will answer and say, 'Lord, when did we see you hungry or thirsty or a stranger or naked or ill or in prison, and not minister to your needs? He will answer them, 'Amen, I say to you, what you did not do for one of these least ones, you did not do for me,' And these will go off to eternal punishment, but the righteous to eternal life."

(Matt. 25:31-46)

THE MURAL

Holy Cross Church

There are times when tragedy, death, and illness can test your faith in God. While looking forward to retirement after the Apollo Space Program ended, I broke my right arm, elbow, and wrist. I had always dreamed of pursuing my art career and opening an art gallery. Now my painting hand was in poor condition.

As soon as I retired and recuperated, I painfully took up my brush and tried to paint left handed. It was possible that my right hand would never be the same, for I had lost some of my control after the operation. But even though the injury to the elbow was permanent, my fingers were able to handle the brush and palette. With much patience and determination, I struggled to overcome my handicap.

While I was thinking about my unfortunate situation and recuperating from my painful condition, my wife suddenly was rushed to the hospital, had a serious operation, and died twelve days later. My dream seemed shattered. I was left with a small retirement and four children, all attending Catholic schools with three tuitions to be paid. My youngest was seven years old, and I woke up a widower with an uncertain future ahead.

It is easy to love God when things are going well. How would I love Him when He sends crosses for me to bear, especially the death of a loved one? Up to this time, I had tried hard to keep the family going, being a good father and husband. With the loss of one's helpmate, faith can be

Holy Cross Church in San Jose, California.

shaken and trials drain the spirit. A great change came over me as I saw the world in a different light. Now I was alone with all the family responsibilities. I knew that I had to make major adjustments without my wife at my side. Things did not look too bright.

With circumstances so dark and gloomy, it was my

Catholic faith that carried me through these trying times. It was the lowest period of my life. Turning to the faith that I lived, I refused to despair. My Lord, Jesus Christ, continued at my side, in the Mass, in receiving Him in Holy Communion, and in the wonderful wealth of friends who came to help and comfort me. It brought me closer to God than ever before, for I accepted His will. God gives and God takes, and time will heal my sorrow. MY LIFE WILL GO ON.

An event occurred later that resulted in reaffirming the truth of my Faith. The Holy Name Society at my parish Church, Holy Cross in San Jose, California, asked me to paint a religious scene on a bare ceiling above the main altar. Mr. Joe Sunseri recommended me to Father Adolph Nalin, the pastor. The challenge overwhelmed me. I had no experience in mural painting, only in landscape in oils. Knowing my limitations, I determined in gratitude to God and in memory of my late wife to go ahead and do my best. God gave me this talent and wanted me to use it.

Father Nalin granted me permission to choose an appropriate subject to paint. I chose the Ascension of Christ into heaven. The painting would not be an artistic work for critics, but a sincere attempt to express my love for Christ as best as possible with my limited talent.

The painting depicts Jesus going to His home in heaven. This theme would remind the viewer of the supernatural truth that we are a pilgrim people here on earth, destined to reach our eternal home in heaven. Christ is the way, the truth, and the life. Below is the altar, where the Sacrifice of the Mass is offered. Here the people of God

Holy Cross Church today.

gather each Sunday to worship Him. They adore their Creator, receive Jesus in Holy Communion, and they receive the grace to carry them through life's journey to the promised land of eternal happiness.

The sky is blue and cheerful with fleecy clouds floating above; Christ is rising with arms outstretched as an invitation to those below in the congregation, appearing to say, in my Father's house are many dwelling places prepared for you. Above Christ is a dove, the symbol of the Holy Spirit proclaiming this is my beloved Son in whom I am well pleased. Higher above the Holy Spirit is the hand of God the Father completing the unity of the blessed Trinity. I wanted people to reflect on the reality of life from earth to heaven.

Lacking the technical skill to paint directly on the ceiling, I came up with a way to achieve the same result. I painted eight large canvas panels in oil. After four months of burying myself in painting the many details I completed the project. Then Nick Ferraro and James Wilson glued the panels to the ceiling.

A remarkable incident happened on the final day of completion. I needed to touch up the clouds in the sky, and had climbed the ladder behind the altar, when suddenly I heard gentle sobbing in the last row of pews. I turned around and observed a Mexican woman with her head buried in her hands. She was a lonely figure in the empty church.

I felt sorry for her. Climbing down, I walked over softly and asked her if I could be of any help. With tears in

her eyes she told me her father was dying of cancer. "What can I do?" she implored. It so happened that my father had just died recently of throat cancer, and I knew how she felt. I consoled her with my vision of faith, and urged her to resign to God's will. Death is not the end, I said, just look at that painting. I explained in detail what I had done. See Jesus ascending to heaven? He has a place prepared for your father! Your father is going to his true home. Christ will be with him for all eternity. Have faith. She gazed at

I painted eight large canvas panels in oil.

Photo by Father Nalin

Nick Ferraro and James Wilson glued the panels to the ceiling

Photo by Father Nalin

Photo by Father Nalin

the panorama of the mural, and I quietly went back to finish my painting.

Barely a week went by, and on a Saturday morning I returned to Holy Cross Church to review the painting once again. A funeral was in progress. I stood aside watching in respect. A black limousine pulled alongside the curb. A woman in black stepped out, helped by someone, and she spotted me. She left the group, came straight to me, hugged me, and cried, "Thank you! Thank you!" It was the woman I had tried to comfort the week before, whose father was dying of cancer. This was his last farewell. The painting, she said, eased her sorrow, and now her father is going to his God.

With a lump in my throat, I bowed and thanked God, feeling rather humbled. Although the mural was not perfect, my efforts in painting it were not in vain. I felt the emotional impact that she experienced, for I, too, went and viewed it again, this time with the eyes of faith. There was

Christ with arms stretched out, looking down on me as if He were saying, "Come, I have a place for you." With the help of His grace, I hope to keep myself worthy of His love, and keep my eyes on the goal, the vision of God in heaven.

It was a startling surprise for the parishioners when they viewed the painting for the first time at Sunday Mass. The previous week, the ceiling above the altar had been bare and plain. Suddenly a colorful panorama of Christ ascending on a cloud unfolded before them. One of the viewers must have been moved by the scene, for I received this beautiful letter a few days later:

March 14-15, 1977

Dear Mr. Quartuccio:

I wish to compliment you and also to thank you for the beautiful oil painting you completed on the ceiling of the Sanctuary of Holy Cross Church. It was like looking into a brilliant ray of sunshine upon entering the church last Sunday morning and seeing this beautiful painting for the first time. I know that my eyes were directed upward during most of the Mass, for it embodied what my thoughts have always been of Our Lord's welcome to his Beloved Son as He ascended into the Kingdom of Heaven. I am very sure that many others entertained that same beautiful thought.

Mr. Joe Sunseri's presentation address was inspiring and beautiful and uplifting. It was a Mass and an occasion that we all long shall remember. The beauty of it all is that the lovely painting will always remain in the Sanctuary of Holy Cross Church as a monument to your devotion and talent and love of real and inspiring art.

Most sincerely,
Mrs. Edmund C. Flynn

MY GOAL: GOD IN HEAVEN

One cold, starry night on top of Mount Hamilton, California, I visited the Lick Observatory with the rest of my junior high school astronomy class to view the moon and the planet Saturn. I was thrilled at the view of the craters on the moon and the rings around Saturn. While walking around the huge dome of the observatory, I gazed at the stars and wondered what lies beyond that vast space and distance?

I was young and could not grasp the immensity of the universe. I wanted to live forever so I could wander through

the galaxy and see the mysteries of space. I yearned to see Mars, Jupiter, Saturn, and experience the limitlessness of time and eternity. That dream stays with me to this day.

Years later I worked for NASA at Ames Research, and lived to see some of the dream come true. Men reached the moon, and I saw the moon rocks that the astronauts brought back. I made sand targets in the Planetology Branch to advance the study of meteor craters for the Apollo Project in the race to the moon. But even with dramatic advancements in space exploration, I still felt that something was missing; I was not completely satisfied. Nothing short of seeing God would fulfill my happiness.

*"My being thirsts for God, the living God.
When can I go and see the face of
God?"*
(Psalm 42-43:3)

The great Saint Augustine said in his confessions many centuries ago that God made us for Himself, and that our hearts will never be at rest, until they rest in Him.

This quest for God continues until I finally rest in Him in eternity. The joy of knowing Him will only be fulfilled in reality in the beautiful vision of MY CREATOR. There my heart will be at rest, at home, supremely joyful and happy.

Someday I hope to see God as He is, face to face. There will be no more frustrations, no more worries, no sickness, only total happiness. My heart and mind will be completely full, and will be working at their highest according to the graces I have attained in life.

My mind will never be filled with knowing until I can truly know, love, and possess God. I want to know God with all the power that I have, for in Him is the real joy, peace, and happiness that I seek.

My soul will grow in grace while on earth, and at death whatever capacity it has stretched to will be filled with glory and joy in heaven. Whether I be a thimbleful of happiness, or a barrelful of happiness, I will be completely overflowing with happiness. My soul will shine like a diamond in the sky.

The me who in this world struggled to love God and neighbor, will be the same me loving God for all eternity, with all the Saints, friends, and relatives who also attained their destiny in heaven.

In heaven, I will be in the changeless now of God. Time will be no more. My knowledge of all things will be perfect. My earthly body will rise again in glory — perfect, beautiful. My eyes are on that goal, union with Christ in heaven.

> *"What eye has not seen, and ear has not heard,*
> *and what has not entered the human heart,*
> *what God has prepared for those who love him."*
>
> (1 Cor. 2:9)

EPILOGUE

As I look back and reflect on the world and the condition of humanity, I have to conclude that only God's grace can rescue us from our sinfulness. If people do not seek the truth, then falsehood and untruth will dominate our lives, leaving in their wake ruin, misery, and destruction.

In striving for peace, joy, and happiness, I find that I must create my happiness by conquering my bad habits and evil inclinations. I must try to be Christlike, with the purity of intention to be humble in all circumstances. I must know myself: my strengths, my weaknesses. Because negative thinking destroys peace of soul, I try to look on the bright side of life.

Most of all, I try to be realistic and live one day at a time. Yesterday is gone, and tomorrow is yet to come. Today is my immediate concern. I must avoid self-pity and idleness, and have self-esteem, using my talents wisely to the best of my ability. Christ says to me:

> *"Do not worry about tomorrow; tomorrow will take care of itself. Sufficient for a day is its own evil."*
> (Matt. 6:34)

I am more convinced now than ever before that all who seek the truth of life and their eternal destination will find the fullness of faith in the One, Holy, Catholic, Apostolic Church. No other church is able to claim these four marks. In the Catholic Church, I find the authority, infallibility, and indefectibility that I seek. Christ gave His word that He is the Way, the Truth, and the Life.

Christ The Pantocrator
The Cathedral of Monreale in Sicily, Italy.

Anthony Quartuccio

Artist and Author

A native of Sicily, Anthony Quartuccio came to the United States when he was seven years old. He has lived most of his life in California's Santa Clara Valley, and currently resides in the central coast city of Paso Robles.

His artistic interest developed early. He had formal training at Jean Turner Art School in San Francisco, as well as private studies with various artists in the Bay Area. Most of his technique, however, is the result of his own study and experimentation, inspired by years of international travels. Working primarily in the media of oil and acrylic, he uses the brush and palette knife to express his style. He has chosen landscapes, farms, deserts and western scenes as his prime subjects.

As a result of his love for Baja California and Mexico, Quartuccio has traveled extensively painting and collecting sketches of nature's beauty. Among his sketches and paintings of his travels are some depicting the remote missions of San Borja and San Javier. He strives to capture the illusion of reality with paint and brush for the enjoyment of others.

As an author and illustrator, Quartuccio was first published in the San Jose Mercury at age fifteen. His most recent books include: Rambling through Baja California with Pen and Brush, Tony's Guide to Better Painting, Santa Clara Valley: an Artist's View, and illustrations for The Saints of the California Landscape.

Quartuccio's paintings appear in private collections in the San Francisco Bay Area, Lake Tahoe, Colorado Springs, Australia and Italy. He has won many outstanding awards including the "People's Choice Award," and is in the 13th edition of Who's Who in California.

While painting a mural of the "Ascension of Christ into heaven" above the altar of Holy Cross Church in San Jose, California, and reflecting on his Catholic faith, he made a pledge to write of his convictions and to share his faith with others. Peace, joy and happiness spring from his heart in the love of God.

Other books by Anthony Quartuccio

Tony's Guide to Better Painting

Rambling Through Baja California With Pen & Brush

Santa Clara Valley —An Artist's View Today & Yesterday

Saints of the California Landscape — by Raymund Wood

(Illustrated by Anthony Quartuccio)